Twentieth Century
Furniture

TWENTIETH CENTURY FURNITURE

Grange BOOKS

A QUANTUM BOOK

Published by Grange Books
an imprint of Grange Books Plc
The Grange
Kingsnorth Industrial Estate
Hoo, nr. Rochester
Kent ME3 9ND

1-84013-281-7

This book is produced by
Quantum Books Ltd
6 Blundell Street
London N7 9BH

Project Manager: Rebecca Kingsley
Project Editor: Judith Millidge
Designer: Wayne Humphries
Editor: Clare Haworth-Maden

The material in this publication previously appeared in
Encyclopedia of Furniture

QUM20FT
Set in Times
Reproduced in Singapore by Eray Scan (Pte) Ltd
Printed in Singapore by Star Standard Industries (Pte) Ltd

CONTENTS

INTRODUCTION

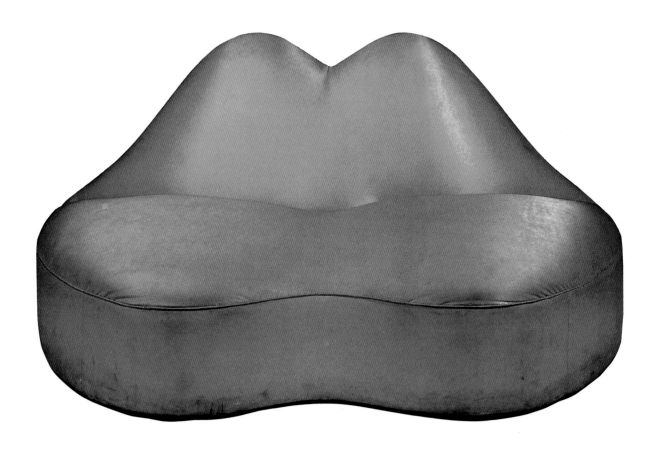

One of the interesting features about the evolution of furniture styles is the history that has developed alongside it; the external social developments, political and financial phenomena, the changes in style according to functional use and necessity, and the artistic tastes of different cultures. The rapid development of man-made materials during the course of the last two centuries has radically quickened the pace of change, adding inspiration to the interpretations of individual craftsmen and innovators who have played an essential role in refining and reassessing furniture design. Indeed, the combination of function and traditional use, and the craftsmanship, techniques and materials used are all relevant to the way furniture shapes and designs have changed and developed over the years and continue to do so today.

Opposite page: 'Mae West hot-lips sofa' based on a design by Salvador Dali, 1936–7. This sofa is a classic example of the way a piece of furniture can be used to express an artistic concept more dramatically than a purely decorative object.

Below: French Art Nouveau corner table with tea tray by Hector Guimard, c. 1900. This walnut table has a matching tea tray with a bronze handle, and is typical of the chic Parisian school of Art Nouveau.

There was a wide variety of furniture styles struggling for acceptance in fashionable circles at the beginning of the twentieth century. Art Nouveau, which was extremely popular in France at the end of the nineteenth century, was more widely adopted in Europe and America in the early years of the twentieth century. With its decorative, curvilinear features, however, it was not suited to mass-production, and declined after World War I.

Function, rather than form became all-important, a concept that was full developed after 1920. In the years preceding World War I, experimental designers such as Charles Rennie Mackintosh, Joseph Hoffmann, and Koloman Moser produced some highly individual furniture which was stylistically influential without being functionally revolutionary.

Functionalism had its philosophical roots in the eighteenth century, but in the first quarter of the twentieth century designers realised that beauty and fitness for purpose could be united. Architects were the first to adopt this idea, and the architectural styles of Louis Sullivan,

Frank Lloyd Wright, and Le Corbusier naturally extended to the way their buildings were furnished.

In Europe, one of the leading influences on functional design was the Bauhaus, the German craft school founded by the architect Walter Gropius at Weimar in 1919. Before its demise in 1933, the Bauhaus established modern design standards compatible with machine production.

EARLY TWENTIETH CENTURY FRENCH DESIGN
The great Paris Exposition of 1900 was dominated by the Art Nouveau style, and many leading Parisian cabinet-makers produced items in a debased version of Art Nouveau. A reaction set in almost immediately, and several designers began to work in a more restrained manner, drawing their inspiration from eighteenth century neo-classicism and French country furniture.

ART DECO
The restrained, understated features of the style that came to be known as Art Deco caught the

Below right: Art Deco salon suite, c. 1925. Designed by André Mare and Louis Süe this suite was exhibited in Paris in 1925 at the Exposition des Arts Decoratifs.

Below: A French chair by René Herbst, c. 1930. This chair is one of a series of chairs with chrome frames and expandable elastic stretched across. It shows typical minimalist design of classic simplicity and function.

public imagination in 1925. The name derives from the Exposition des Arts Decoratifs et Industriels Modernes held in Paris in 1925, which promoted a sumptuous, low-slung look in interior design, characterised by gleaming veneer, exotic materials and crackle lacquer, combined with chrome and steel.

The elegance and opulence of Parisian Art Deco were best expressed in the stunning interiors of the 1920s and 1930s, often the collaboration between furniture and textile designers, sculptors, painters, lacquer-workers and other talented artists and artisans. The ensemblier came to the fore with such names as Emile-Jacques Ruhlmann, Robert Mallet Stevens (1866–1958), Eileen Gray

(1878–1976,) Francis Jourdain (1876–1958), Louis Süe (1875–1968) and André Mare (1887–1932), who founded the Compagnie des Arts Français, taking on the formidable task of creating a total design, or ensemble, for a room, including the wall, window and floor coverings, furniture and other co-ordinating accessories.

MODERNISM AND POST MODERNISM

From the very start, Art Deco had comprised two extremes of style. In France where the movement had evolved high style Art Deco manifested itself emotionally with exuberance, colour and playfulness. Elsewhere in Europe and America it was interpreted more intel-

lectually, with designers basing their work on theories of functionalism and economy.

In 1926 a loosely-knit band of French Modernists – Francis Jourdain, Pierre Chareau, Le Corbusier, Robert Mallet-Stevens and René Herbst – had become increasingly outspoken in their criticism of Art Deco designers, who catered to select clients by creating elaborately crafted unique pieces. The Modernists argued that the new age required excellent design for everyone, and that quality and mass production were not mutually exclusive concepts. Modernism made rapid progress in the late 1920s, although most designers took a stance somewhat short of the severe factionalism espoused by its ardent adherents.

The partnerships of Jean-Michel Frank (1887–1941) and Adophe Chanaux (1887–1965) produced some of the most original design form their studio on Paris. In 1927 Frank commissioned Chanaux to decorate his apartment to his own designs and so began a professional association that ended only with Frank's suicide in New York shortly after the outbreak of World War II. The two sometimes collaborated with their immediate neighbours, including Salvador Dali, Alberto and Diego Giacometti and Pablo Picasso, and among their well-known patrons were Mr and Mrs Nelson Rockefeller, Elsa Schiaparelli and Templeton Crocker. The partnership's furniture was known for it extreme sparseness and simplicity

of line and function. On visiting Frank's apartments, Jean Cocteau remarked that it was a pity that burglars had taken everything.

BRITISH DESIGNERS

The designs of Charles Voysey (1857–1941) are among the most innovative in the entire history of English furniture. Characteristic features of his work include tall, narrow uprights, broad flat cornices, and large strap hinges with cut-out decoration. His furniture was made of oak sometimes stained, and produced by accomplished craftsmen such as Arthur Simpson which subsequently made furniture to his own designs in a style derived from Voysey's.

The furniture made by the Bedford firm of J.P. White to designs by M.H. Baillie Scott (1865–1945) was more elaborately decorated than Voysey's. Most pieces were inlaid with stylised flowers or birds, but the forms, however, were quite simple. Some pieces designed by Baillie-Scott for the grand ducal palace at Darmstadt in 1897 were made up by cabinet-makers at the Guild of Handicraft (founded in 1888 by Charles Ashbee).

Around the turn of the century several manufactures, such as Liberty & Co Wylie & Lockhead of Glasgow and John Dollie Henry produced furniture in a style often called 'quaint' by contemporaries and loosely based on the work of designers of the Arts and Crafts Movement. Other manufacturers producing similar furniture were the Bath Cabinet-makers Company (for which Ellwood did some designs) and the London firm of Shapland & Peter. One furnishing company, Heals & Son of London, produced a wide variety of furniture in Cotswold style created by Gimson and Barnsley. It was designed by Ambrose Heal (1872–1959) and was featured in the

Below right: French 'Tables Gigogne' by Franck and Chanaux, c. 1935.Gigogne means 'mother of many children'. These tables were originally created in oak and covered in vellum with straw marquetry.

Below: An English sitting room with Chesterfield sofa by Heal & Son, 1920s. This sitting room was designed by Ambrose Heal and the illustration is by Palmer-Jones from a contemporary magazine.

Top right: English Bedroom suite, 1912–18. Designed by the Omega Workshops, this room is far removed from the opulent French Art Deco style. The furniture does, however, feature stylised flowers and leaves, not unlike those found on contemporary pieces by Jean Dunand.

company's 1899 catalogue of 'Simple Furniture', which featured items more modest in scale intended for suburban homes.

OMEGA WORKSHOPS
In 1913 Roger Fry (1866–1934) established the Omega Workshops in London to produce painted pottery and tin-glazed earthenware. Fry wanted to involve artists in the design of furniture, carpets and textiles, as well as ceramics, and the workshop produced furniture designed by, among others Vanessa Bell and Duncan Grant (Fry's fellow directors) Wyndham Lewis, Nina Hammett, Edward Wadsworth and William Roberts. The furniture was painted or decorated in marquetry, in aggressively modern styles base on Fauvism.

FROM UTILITY TO POST-MODERNISM
World War II set its own limitations on furniture design just as World War I had, and in Britain in 1942 it led to government intervention in the furniture industry in the form of the Utility Furniture Scheme. Between 1943 and 1952 only approved designs could be manufactured. The Utility furniture that resulted – plain, unpretentious pieces – was intended to help the furnishing of bombed homes. In the sense, it was a combination of the spirit of the Arts and Crafts movement with the techniques and materials of mass production. The forms would have found favour with Ernest Gimson or Ernest and Sidney Barnsley, although the materials would not. Some of the designs of the Utility range were produced by a design panel, chaired by Sir Gordon Russell (1892–1980)

A new generation of designers, emerged after 1945 who eagerly grasped the challenges offered by a variety of new materials. By the 1960s, however, the main technological changes, the use of plastics and new materials, had given a hitherto unknown freedom to structures, and designers such as Charles Eames and Vico Magistretti were not slow to exploit the possibilities.

The 1960s also saw a marketing revolution

which was represented, if not begun by the Englishman Sir Terence Conran, with his Habitat shop and the Habitat catalogue which first appeared in 1971. The notion of selling furniture in kit form to be assembled at home was not a new one; Gerrit Rietveld and Bauhaus designers had used this technique 50 years before. Mass-production was not new either – Giles Grendey and Thomas Chippendale, for instance has employed vast workshops in the eighteenth century, and the Thonet brothers produced many millions of bentwood chairs in the nineteenth century. However, the Conran combination of high volume production sold in kit form by means of catalogue soon became tremendously popular.

GERMANY

The term for Art Nouveau in Germany was 'Jugendstil' (youth style). In Munich during the late 1890s, a number of architects, painters and sculptors including Hermann Obrist (1863-1927), August Endell (1871-1921) Richard Reimerschmid (1868-1957), Bernhard Pankok (1872-1943) and Bruno Paul (1874-1968), turned their attention to the applied arts. In 1897 these five among others founded the Vereinigte Werkstätten für Kunst im Handwerk (United Workshop for Art in the Handicrafts). Obrist and Endell designed furniture in flowing natural forms that were determined by a theory of interaction between physical appearances and psychological reactions. Obrist's furniture was made of oak, and Endell's of elm. Pankok's designs were also based on natural forms, using oak, spruce pearwood and walnut.

The work of the Belgian designer Henri Van de Velde (1863-1957) made a considerable impact on the Munich artists. Van de Velde used lines to express psychological moods, an intellectual approach which appealed to the Germans.

GERMAN WORKSHOPS

One of the intentions underlying the work of the Munich artists was to create furniture cheap enough for the majority of the ordinary public to buy. The Germans took into account the new woodworking machines that were being developed. The leader of this tendency was the cabinet-marker Karl Schmidt, (1873–1948) Reimerschmid's brother-in-law, who in 1898 opened the Dresdner Werkstätten (Dresden Workshop).

In 1902 the artist Adelbert Niemeyer and the upholsterer Karl Bertsch founded a workshop in Munich for the manu-

Left: A chair by Vico Magistretti. A classic Milanese chair which relies on simple elements and yet has a stark, sculptural quality.

Below: Illustration from the first Habitat catalogue, 1971.

Below right: German sideboard, oak, c. 1900. August Endell based his designs on the psychological effects of line and proportion, and he believed the shape alone could induce feelings of serenity and satisfaction. His decorative motifs were derived from illustrations in scientific books dealing with primitive life forms.

Below: Chairs by Josef Hoffmann. From a set of six, the design of these chairs emphasises simplicity and respect for tradition.

facture of furniture. In 1907 it merged with the Dresdner Werkstätten to become the Deutsche Werkstätten (not to be confused with the Deutsche Werkbund, promoted by the German government and founded in the same year). Niemeyer continued to design furniture for the Deutsche Werkstätten until his death. Other designers who occasionally worked for the Dresden concern were Baillie Scott and the Austrians Josef Hoffmann and Koloman Moser.

DARMSTADT DESIGNERS

In 1897 Grand Duke Ernst Ludwig of Hesse-Darmstadt encouraged the establishment of an artists' colony at Matildenhohe on the outskirts of Darmstadt and gave some land for the project. Seven artists were invited to join the colony. Along with M.H.Baillie Scott, was Peter Behrens (1868–1940), a painter and architect who had been working in Munich during the 1890s. Also invited was Hans Christiansen (1866–1945) who designed pieces in a geometrical style, decorated with inlaid patterns, marquetry, or low relief silver

plaques. Josef Maria Olbrich (1867–1908) was an Austrian architect who started his career in Vienna and became one of the leading figures of the Secession. In 1899, he arrived at the colony where he went on to create furniture in a style that was a successful blend of organic shapes and geometrical ornament.

ART DECO IN GERMANY

Art Deco has come to be so closely associated with France, and to a lesser degree Britain, and America, that it easy to overlook the fact that the decorative arts were thriving in Weimar Germany. The demand for basic items for the home continued – the German porcelain and ceramic industries were the largest in Europe between the wars, for example. Companies like Villeroy and Boch in Dresden flourished by meeting the realities of the economic situation. After 1933 with Hitler's rise to power, tsome of the best German designers emigrated to America, mostly via London.

BAUHAUS

The work of the Bauhaus (founded by Walter

Gropius in 1919) helped to create the Modern Movement. Influential designers included Marcel Breuer (1902–81) and Mies van der Rohe (1886–1969)who experimented with the avant garde. Breuer left Hungary to study painting in Vienna and in 1924 he took charge of the Bauhaus workshop concerned with interior design. He encouraged the students to produce in simple materials, in keeping with the principles of originality and function.

AUSTRIA

In Austria the Art Nouveau style was called 'Secessionstil', after the Vienna Secession which was formed in 1897. A group of architects, painters and sculptors seceded from the official artists' organisation and held their own exhibition in the Secessionhaus. One of the older Secessionists was the architect Otto Wagner (1841–1918), who designed some very plain furniture for his buildings. It was manufactured by the firm of Thonet brothers, which had pioneered the technology of bentwood furniture.

Another Viennese architect, Adolf Loos (1870–1933) designed bentwood chairs manu-

factured by Thonet for the Café Museum. Loos had been impressed by the work of the English Arts and Crafts Movement and several of the pieces he designed were of simple, panelled construction. His work is marked by elegant proportions and a judicious disposition of simple reeding and metal fittings. Loos himself criticised its members for the ornament and deliberate artiness of much of the furniture they displayed

WIENER WERKSTÄTTE

The principal Secession designers were two young architects, Joseph Hoffmann (1870–1956) and Koloman Moser (1868–1918), who produced furniture that later became severely rectangular. In 1903 Hoffmann and Moser founded the Wiener Werkstätte (Vienna Workshop). Much of Hoffmann's inventive furniture designs show the influence of Charles Rennie Mackintosh.

ITALY

Italy made a unique contribution to the history of furniture through the work of Carlo Bugatti

Above: German cabinet and chair, c. 1900. Designed at Darmstadt by Josef Maria Olbrich. The marquetry on the cabinet doors shows the influence of the English Arts and Crafts designer M.H. Baillie Scott.

Left: The Laccio table by Marcel Breuer, c. 1925. This table is elegant and striking, with a combination of glass and chrome, and is obviously from the same design spirit as the Wassily chair.

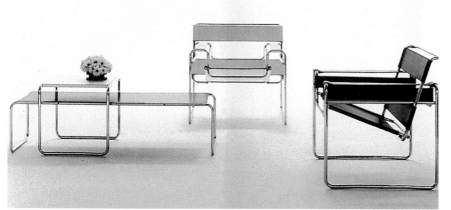

Below: Italian drawing room furniture, wood, metal and vellum, 1900. The Moorish style of this furniture, designed by Carlo Bugatti, exhibits the eclectic aproach to styles and materials employed by this idiosyncratic Italian designer.

(1856–1940), the father of the sports car designer. Bugatti originally trained as an architect before opening his first furniture workshop and outlet in Milan in the 1880s. He also produced silver jewellery and other goods.

Around 1900, the Italian architect Ernesto Basile (1857–1932) created furniture in the Art Nouveau style which was known in Italy as 'Stile Liberty' or 'stile floreale'. The elegant forms of Basile's furniture are decorated with carved foliate ornament. Basile who was primarily an architect, became chief designer for Vittoria Ducarto's firm, a sizeable interior design workshop in Palermo, Sicily. They designed extensively in Art Nouveau style, as well as in some more prestigious projects, exhibiting at Italian fairs in the early years of the century. Overall, however, the first work was commercial and the firm produced good

quality, stylish furniture such as that of the Grand Hotel Palermo, for general use. Also influential in this style was cabinet-maker Carlo Zen ,whose Art Nouveau furniture, which often has a dual function, is elaborately carved with floral decoration.

POSTWAR ITALIAN DESIGN

Although the Milan School was responsible for countless innovative ideas many have not endured well. The influence of its premier exponent, the innovative designer Carlo Mollino, can be seen in the work of Carlo Graffi, especially his juxtaposition of material, such as wood and glass. Swiss-born Alberto Giacometti (1901–66) trained in Italy in the 1920s and was greatly influenced by the Romanian-born sculptor Constantin Brancusi (1876–1957).

Ettore Sottsass (b.1917) is widely regarded as the most outstanding Italian designer of his generation.and was a pioneer of postwar reconstruction. His most important work was produced in the 1980s by the Milanese group known as Memphis.

THE NETHERLANDS

Most Dutch furniture of the early twentieth century was simple, although the work of K.P.C. de Bazel and J.L.M. Lauweiks was sometimes decorated with carved motifs derived from Egyptian or Assyrian art. The best known designer of the period was Gerrit Rietveld (1888-1964). Rietveld, the son of a cabinet-maker, established his own furniture workshop in 1911. His early work were handcrafted, in keeping with the Dutch Arts and Crafts tradition. In 1916 he designed the Red-Blue chair, its formal and spatial innovations no doubt inspired by Rietveld's recent encounters with new materials and forms.

SCANDINAVIA

Reflecting contemporary Scandinavian interest in traditional folk culture, the furniture was simply constructed and often painted or carved with animal or floral motifs. In Sweden J.A.G. Acke and Carl Westman designed pieces that featured the curving rhythmic lines of Van der Velde, while Carl Bergsten's designs were influenced by the Wiener Werkstätte.

During the first two decades of the century, the Norwegian Gabriel Kielland, the Dane Kaare Klin (1888–1954) and the Swede Carl Malmsten designed elegant, good quality furniture. The Finnish designers Louis Sparre, Eliel Saarinen (1873–1950) and Eero Saarinen (1910–61) were pioneers of the international Modern Movement and their work reflects a preoccupation with construction and function.

As a furniture designer the Finnish Alvar Aalto, (1898–1976) one of the most prolific designers of modern times, rejected new materials, such as metals and plastic. Comparisons have been drawn between Aalto's laminated birch and the moulded plywood produced in the 1930s by, for example, Summer and Eames. The difference is that Aalto makes the structure work in the design, producing an integrated whole that is also elegant.

AMERICA

The influence of the many Chicago-based architect-teachers who taught the young Frank Lloyd Wright can be detected in the writings and work of the Prairie School. George Grant Elmslie (1872–1952) and George Washington Maher drew heavily on medieval and Renaissance traditions, using scrolls, carvings of animal heads, and deep arm- and back-rests of sixteenth century European designs, but in combination with the sturdy woods and rugged individualism of the Midwest.

MISSION FURNITURE

The impact of the British Art and Crafts ideas on American designers is perhaps best seen in the work and philosophy of Gustav Stickley (1857–1946). Stickley began working in a relative's chair factory in 1876, and in 1899 he formed the Gustav Stickley Co. in Eastwood outside Syracuse, New York. His furniture, made in native hardwoods, was intended to evoke the 'simple life' of the early pioneers. Its success and easy adaptability to machine production meant that he had many competitors, including two of his brothers, who founded a rival company in 1902.

New York state was also the home of the community of craftsmen headed by Elbert Hubbard (1856–1915) and working in East 'Aurora. Known as the Roycrofters', they concentrated on the simplest pieces – oak

Below: An American Arts and Crafts oak hall bench, c. 1910. Typical of Gustav Stickley's work, this bench was made from locally-available woods in order to ensure that it was cheap enough for middle-class Americans.

benches, tables, chairs, and bookcases. The dark, austere work of the two New York groups has become known as Mission Furniture because it was designed with 'with a mission to perform'.

AMERICAN ART DECO

Furniture ran the gamut from variation on both the high-style French and functionalist Le Corbusier schools, to small-scale architectonic essays and blatant neo-classical designs. Paul T. Frankl, whose 1930 cry ' Ornament –crime' was taken up by many American designers, created distinctive skyscraper bookcases and cabinets, with stepped section and intricate compartments. Kem Weber and J.B. Peters, two Los Angeles designers also adapted the skyscraper style to their tall pieces, and Chicago-based Abel Faidy produced a leather settee with a whimsical design derived from architecture for a private apartment that could have been custom-built for Radio City.

The metal and wood furniture of Frank Lloyd Wright was not as severe as that of the Bauhaus. For instance he enamelled in warm russet brown the steel frames of his famous desk and chair from 1936–9. Known as Cherokee Red, it was designed for the S.C. Johnson & Son building in Racine, Wisconsin, so that the colour would complement the American walnut of the chair arms and desk top and the brown upholstery.

Eliel Saarinen, Eugene Schoen, Wolfgang Hoffmann, Gilbert Rohde and Joseph Urban were among the many designers who applied theirs talents to creating furniture for the American market. On the whole, their pieces were sturdy, mass-produced and distinctly modernist, some with echoes of French, German, and Viennese design, others uniquely American in form, colour and materials. Aluminium, chromium and other metal furni-

ture were in the ascendancy, but wooden pieces continued to be popular. Synthetic materials such as Formica and Lucite were already used in furniture design. An armchair by Elsie de Wolf, its traditional scrolled back design moulded of Lucite, demonstrates a strange but witty meeting of old and new

MODERNISM AND POST MODERNISM

After World War II, American design flourished with an influx of talented craftsmen and designers such as Walter Gropius and Eliel Saarinen. Saarinen's son Eero, and Charles Eames (1907–78) worked with plastics, fibreglass and moulds in ways that have since been imitated and adapted throughout the world. In southern California, the architect Charles Summer Greene (1886–1957) and his brother Henry Mather Greene (1870-1954) created furniture to complement their grand Spanish-style mansions, producing pieces in rich woods such as walnut, cedar, and Honduras mahogany inlaid with fruitwood and precious stones.

From the 1930s, Charles Eames was perhaps the most important twentieth century designer. The streamlined school of the Art Deco period was exemplified by industrial designers such as Raymond Loewy (1893–1987) Walter Dorwin Teague (1883–1960) and Walter von Nelson who helped to define modern culture with their tableware, hardware and household appliances. Important designers of recent years have included George Nelson (b.1907) Harry Bertoia (b. 1915), Danny Lane, Floris van den Broecke, Eric de Graaff and Philippe Starcke.

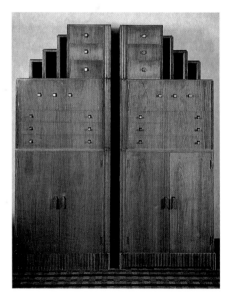

Below: America chests of drawers, walnut, c. 1928. These chests of drawers, which have ebony trim and green-lacquered interiors, were designed by Paul T. Frankl in the skyscraper style – architectonic pieces that were intended to be at home in high-rise urban apartments.

CHAIRS AND SOFAS

Not all new furniture in the early twentieth century was modern in styling. The Edwardians commissioned many fine pieces in Sheraton and Adam styles, and these fashionable revivals were reflected in commercial ranges. New forms did begin to appear, however, which were sleeker and restrained. This new style, which has since become known as Art Deco, was characterised by luxurious decorative furniture, with large expanses of gleaming veneer, exotic materials and crackle lacquer combined with bright chrome and steel. Art Deco was modern because it used aspects of machine design as inspiration, although it might also be seen as the final chapter in the craft of cabinet-making. There were two trends: early experiments in furniture-making using metals and plastics intended for mass-production, and high quality craftsmanship in traditional materials.

EUROPEAN TRENDS

The most dominant force in twentieth century chair design was that of northern Europeans – the Scandinavian and Germans. One of the first to design attractive functional furniture for mass production was the German architect Richard Riemerschmid. His chairs were specifically designed for factory production and consisted of several elements produced separately and then nailed together. This radical approach was mirrored by the Dutchman Gerrit Rietveld, a founder member of the De Stijl group of artist-designers. Their belief in using only primary colours and rectangular forms, and a commitment to the 'machine age' led to their continuing influence on modern chair construction through simplicity and lightness.

GERRIT RIETVELD

The best know designer of the early twentieth century was Gerrit Rietveld (1888-1964). Rietveld, the son of a cabinet-maker, was a natural designer. Trained in cabinet-making jewellery and then finally architecture, he

established his own furniture workshop in 1911. His early work was simply and carefully handcrafted, in keeping with the Dutch Arts and Crafts tradition. In 1916, however, he was introduced to the painter Bart van der

Previous page: Norwegian painted chairs by Gerhard Munthe, c. 1911 These delightful fantasy chairs are a virtuoso indulgence of decoration; the sculptural carved mask heads clearly come from Scandinavian folkloric tradition, as does the interlacing strapwork, which has a Gaelic look. The naively carved scene on the back pane doubtless depicts a fairy tale episode. The chairs absorb many different styles, from Arabesque to Regency, all converted into this burst of colour. Here, the new stylistic freedom is productive rather than limiting.

Below: Chairs designed by Gerrit Rietveld, c. 1917 These military chairs are unapologetically functional, made of very simple joints and inexpensive materials which dismantle completely.

Leck, at the at time a member of the Stijl group, and to the architect Robert van t'Hoff who asked him to copy, from photographs, furniture by Frank Lloyd Wright for the Huis ter Huide. 1917 marked the transition between the organic curving Art Nouveau style and crisp, chic Art Deco. Suddenly straight lines appeared and complex shapes from the most simple of techniques coupled with striking colours. The dramatic interplay of straight lines to form patterns was not a wholly new ides – in the 1860s E. W. Godwin, greatly inspired by oriental design, produced geometric household furniture.

The Red-Blue chair was designed a few months after this, its formal and spatial innovations no doubt inspired by Rietveld's recent encounters with new attitudes, materials and form. The chair was, in fact, designed as a personal experiment to demon-

Above: Beugel fauteuil by Gerrit Rietveld 1927. This shows Rietveld's command of diverse materials.

strate that' a thing of beauty, e.g. a spatial object, could be made of nothing by straight machined lines'. Following its illustration in *De Stijl* magazine, it became widely known in avant-garde circles throughout Europe. Its place in the history of modern art cannot be underestimated.

The Berlin chair (1923) is in some ways an even more exaggerated demonstration of Rietveld's belief in the principles of De Stijl; it is much simpler, and used only tones of black and white. Designed for the Dutch pavilion at the Berlin Exhibition in 1923, in some ways it is even more exaggerated. It is free of previous decorative styles such as Gaudi's neo-Baroque, or even earlier eighteenth century designs; in this chair everything is totally functional.

In 1927 Rietveld designed the Beugel Fauteuil which appears to resemble the Red-Blue chair in plywood and tube, but which in fact takes it strength from the integral triangles from which it is formed.

Rietveld produced an extraordinary variety of innovative chair designs, typically planned with mass-production in his mind. Many of his original designs were produced by G.A.Van Der Groenekan, and the Beugel Fauteuil was produced by Metz & Co in the late 1920s. His imagination was seemingly inexhaustible. He produced many single chairs, typically in very simple materials, designed to be mass-produced cheaply. His concern for the method as well as the results of the design led him to create the Birza chair which was cut from a single piece of fibre that was then folded and fixed in a rigid shape. It was designed for the Birza rooms, and interior which took the name of its patron, Dr W Birza. The overall effect shows similarities with the work of Frenchman

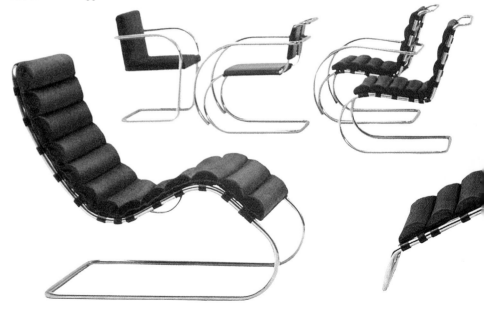

Emile-Jacques Ruhlmann in the shape and sabre legs, and echoes the achievements of the Bauhaus and Scandinavian designers in plywood.

GERMAN DESIGNERS

Richard Reimerschmid's earliest experiments in furniture were some pieces he designed for his own apartment in 1895. They were in the neo-gothic style, made of stained and painted pine, and decorated with elaborate wrought-iron hinges and foliate ornament carved in low relief. However as a result of seeing in 1887 an exhibition in Dresden of Henri Van der Velde's furniture, (whose abstract Art Nouveau style had considerable impact on all the Munich artists),the following year Riemerschmid designed an oak side chair. Its backrests were carried on supports that descended in a sweeping curve to the feet of the front legs.

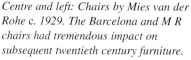
Centre and left: Chairs by Mies van der Rohe c. 1929. The Barcelona and M R chairs had tremendous impact on subsequent twentieth century furniture.

A slightly altered version was soon being sold by Liberty's in London.

BAUHAUS

In Germany the Bauhaus, founded by Walter Gropius in 1919) blossomed within a decade into a force that still influences design today.

Originally headed by Gropius, who later moved to the United States, it encouraged it participants to seek new design answers to problems of material and function. The design of a chair, for example, would be broken down into its most basic components. The work of the Bauhaus helped to create the Modern Movement, and influential designers included Marcel Breuer (1902–81) who designed the important Wassilly chair, and Mies van der Rohe (1889–1969).

The Wassilly chair, designed by Breuer in 1925, is perhaps one of the most famous chairs of the century, and has been in continuous production for nearly 75 years. It took its name from Wassilly Kandinsky, for whose studio it was made at the Bauhaus. This chair, and other

Above and below: Chairs by Josef Hoffmann, c.1905.

His two main chair designs had tremendous impact on subsequent twentieth century furniture. He was born the son of a stone cutter and was apprenticed to the furniture designer and architect, Peter Behrens. He started working for himself in 1912. The Barcelona chair takes its name from the Barcelona International Exhibition for which it was designed, with accompanying ottoman or footstool. Although swiftly conceived, the modernist German pavilion at the exhibition, with its straight lines and minimal encumbrances, was a great success as were the chairs, produced in Berlin and still made by Knoll International today.

Although a director of the Bauhaus from 1930-33, Rohe's furniture designs disregard economy and concentrate on opulence. The flattened steel frame of the Barcelona chair is in fact quote complex, and relatively expensive to produce. He was most famous, however, for his furniture made from tubular

work by Marcel Breuer shows the link between the Dutch De Stijl movement and the Bauhaus. Breuer's early experimentation with tubular chrome chairs led to the countess derivations; Mies van der Rohe, for example, exhibited his Barcelona chair at the Paris Exposition Internationale des Arts Decoratifs et Industriels Modernes of 1925, the showcase of the Art Deco movement. The Bauhaus was the laboratory of the avant-garde.

As political difficulties came to dog the Bauhaus in the 1930s, Breuer moved to England where he helped the firm Isokon to develop designs using sculptured plywood, again sparking off an entirely new generation of furniture.

MIES VAN DER ROHE

Ludwig Mies van der Rohe (1886–1969) was an influential designer of the German Bauhaus.

steel, generally chromed and close to an original design by Mart Stam, which consisted of a continual tube bent to form base, legs, seat, and back. Mies van der Rohe was first to patent the idea, although he claimed that it worked on a different principle to Stam's original. This became the basis of the MR range designed in 1931 with comfort depending on the springing in the tubular frame and the luxurious leather upholsteries. The simple appearance is deceptive, more for aesthetic reasons than structural ones – his famous maxim was that 'God is in the details' – the chair was very carefully designed to give this air of simplicity

WIENER WERKSTÄTTE
In 1903 the Vienna Secession, under the leadership of Josef Hoffmann, transformed itself into the Wiener Werkstätte, whose studios manufactured the Werkstätte's typical grid-like designs, mainly in black and white.

Josef Hoffmann (1870-1952) was an influential architect, closely associate with the Vienna Secession. Although he was radical in his designs, being much influenced by Mackintosh, he was also highly respected and taught at the Vienna School of Arts and Crafts for over 30 years. One of the signatures of his designs is the curious lobes or spheres which supports the joints on the front legs of his chairs. The backs of some chairs are a pastiche of a Sheraton tea tray, decorated with an inlaid fan at the centre. Hoffmann also designed furniture with sharp, geometric motifs, often decorated with grid-like patterns and sometimes studded leather with brass caps to the legs

Although many of his clients were extremely bourgeois Austrians, Hoffmann also published furniture designs under the title 'Simple Furniture', which he considered to be an aspect of good design. Hoffmann was a prolific designer of chairs, some of which

Left: Art Deco salon suite by Maurice Dufresne, c. 1925. This suite uses straight vertical lines to contrast with the gentle horizontal curves, which are echoed under the seat rails and set off the tapestry; the result is not excessive, but still chic.

are faithfully reproduced by Franz Wittmann. The Biach chair shows Hoffmann's command of the bentwood medium as produced by his own factory, Characteristically using geometric shapes, simple straight lines and spherical supports at the joints through which screws join seat to leg, the design was light, economical to produce, yet sturdy and stylish.

FRENCH DESIGN

Art Deco threw up a host of talented and innovative designers in all spheres of the arts including chair design. Pierre Legrain (1889–1929) was influenced by African and Egyptian forms, and he created a variety of original furniture including chairs of carved wood similar to those of ancient Egypt.

Born in Ireland in 1879, Eileen Gray has become known as one of the best individualists of the twentieth century. She trained at the Slade School of Art in London, and then became an apprentice at a lacquer workshop. She worked all over Europe during the next

Above and right: Chairs and stool by Alvar Aalto, laminated wood, c. 1937. The Paimio chair (above) was designed for the Paimio Sanatorium, the first project that brought Aalto to fame. The stacking stool was designed for the Viipuri library around 1930. The simple, functional design was space-saving, an idea which Hoffmann continued with a similar chair which lacked the laminated springy legs made of several leaves of wood. The easy chair is covered with a lattice of webbing, and when fully reclined, resembles a chaise longue.

30 years, with many of the great names of the twentieth century. She was a great Parisian furniture designer and ensemblier, who produced exquisite and hand-made objects such as screens, tables, and chairs, which were often embellished with Japanese Lacquer. She eventually moved to more rectilinear and functional furniture.

LE CORBUSIER

Working in France in the 1920s, Le Corbusier (1887–1965) redefined furniture into three categories – chairs, tables, and shelves- and designed standard pieces for the interiors of his buildings accordingly. Although individual, his chairs show the penchant for 'anonymous' design that pervades the second half of the twentieth century – they are equipment rather than art.

The best known pieces by Le Corbusier are the chairs he designed in collaboration with his cousin Pierre Jeanneret (1896–1967) and Charlotte Perriand (b. 1903). His chaises longues and armchairs, often fashioned of tubular steel frames, and simple, but comfortable and functional leather seats, were slightly more inviting than the spare, minimal designs of the Bauhaus. These, especially the designs of Marcel Breuer and Mies van der Rohe, were even further removed from the plush, upholstered chairs of André Groult (1884–1967) and Maurice Dufrène (1876–1955) which recalled a luxuriant past. Instead, their work clearly signalled a new era in design which still reigns today.

ALVAR AALTO

In Finland, Alvar Aalto (1898–1976) – one of the most prolific designers of modern times

Above: Chairs by Eero Saarinen c. 1955. With the exception of tubular steel furniture and some bentwood designs, most chairs have four legs, which come independently from the seat. Saarinen said of his pedestal design that 'the underside of typical chairs and tables makes a confusing and restless world...I wanted to clear up the slum of legs'. It is hardly surprising that he worked closely with Charles Eames: the fruits of their partnership formed at Cranbrook academy of Art Michigan US are easy to see in his soft-outlined sculptural seats.

– played an interesting role which fell between the traditional craft approach of Scandinavian designers, and the new forms developing in central Europe. As a furniture designer the Finnish Aalto rejected new materials, such as metals and plastic. Convinced that the human body should come in to contact only with natural materials, he utilised laminated birch plywood, moulded to follow human contours. His bentwood forms echo those of the Thonet bothers in nineteenth century France, but belong unmistakably to the twentieth century. In 1939 Aalto founded the firm Artek to produce inexpensive, well-designed textiles, light fittings, and furnishings.

AMERICAN CHANGES
After World War II, American design flour-

ished. Charles Eames (1907-78) is perhaps the most famous of modern chair designers, and is certainly the most collected. He is rightly applauded for two notable achievements: for using plywood which could be permanently moulded in two planes rather than one, and secondly as a designer of truly sculptural chairs.

In 1940 Eames worked with Eero Saarinen to design a range of furniture based on plywood shell which was featured in a competition for organic design in home furnishings, organised by New York's Museum of Modern Art. There is something very European about the outline of these pedestal chairs, which perhaps harks back to Saarinen's European roots. (Born in Finland in 1916, Saarinen spent most of his life in the United States).

Left and below: Oak spindle chairs by Frank Lloyd Wright, c. 1901. These chairs, typical of Wright's furniture, clearly owe a great debt to Charles Rennie Mackintosh. Wright first designed similar chairs for his own dining room, which was very geometric, stark, and fundamentally based on a grid. These chairs are tall (about 5ft) and their undecorated austerity is similar to Japanese design.

FRANK LLOYD WRIGHT

Frank Lloyd Wright (1867–1959) was born in the United States the year before Charles Rennie Mackintosh was born in Scotland, and had a profound influence on American design. Living through all the major styles from the Arts and Crafts Movement though to the 1950s, he subscribed to the holistic design approach which suggested that furniture in the many houses he designed should reflect the shape and spirit of the space which it occupied. He practised this to an almost excessive degree, producing sparse style that architects and designers loved, but which was not particularly practical. Although Wright designed some economy furniture for ordinary use it is obvious that his spindle chairs, for example, use a vast amount of timber and would be

expensive to produce. In spite of this, Frank Lloyd Wright was certainly one of America's most important twentieth century architect-designers, not least for his early treatment of the relationship between furniture and its surroundings.

In the 1920s Wright was commissioned to decorate and furnish the Imperial Hotel in Japan. He insisted on designing everything, including fabric and carpets. The design was minimalist and geometric in lines, based on the hexagon and the octagon and is another example of Wright's desire to first the moveable furniture in to the spirit of the immovable space in which it is contained. The structure itself was built of concrete and so survived the disastrous earthquakes of the '20s before falling prey to property developers in 1968.

Above and left: Oak sidechairs by Frank Lloyd Wright , c. 1920. Designed for the Imperial Hotel in Tokyo, Japan, these chairs use Wright's familiar materials, leather and oak.

Plastic became a commonplace material for furniture in the second half of this century. Its effects on design were crucial moving the emphasis away from decoration and back to fluidity of line. More recent developments show a growing division between designer chairs for the collector and the development of the mass market.

SPAIN

The Spanish architect Antoni Gaudi (1852–1926) created furniture for some of the buildings he designed. He was influence by Viollet-le-Duc and much of his early work was in a neo-gothic style. Between 1885 and 1890 he built a palace in Barcelona for the Güell family for which he designed asym-

metrical furniture in an organic style that prefigures Art Nouveau.

SCOTTISH DESIGNERS

At the end of the nineteenth century Charles Rennie Mackintosh (1868-1928) produced his most famous furniture for Miss Cranston's Tea Rooms in Glasgow. The tall ladder-back chairs were parodies of traditional chairs, and their original shape influenced a generation of designers. He later abandoned Art Nouveau curves and founded the Glasgow School, which concentrated on the line and geometric patterns.

The designer George Walton, (1867–1933) also based in Glasgow until 1898 when he moved to London, gave narrow tapering legs to many of his pieces of furniture. One of his designs was an adaptation of a traditional, rush-seated chair that had arms curving forwards from a narrow back, with a narrow splat back pierced with a heart-shaped opening. This design was widely imitated in both Britain and the rest of Europe.

ITALIAN DESIGNERS

Carlo Bugatti's (1856-1940) chairs and designs for interiors are wonderfully idiosyncratic and difficult to categorise. They drew heavily on the Near East (especially Syria and Egypt) for inspiration in their use of applied and worked metals, such as copper, and the extensive inlay of many different materials, including pewter, ivory and other woods. He had no qualms about mixing different materials and methods. Velum painted with Arabian scenes was used for the seats and backs of his chairs and became one of his trademarks, as did the circle or half finished circle. His work often has chunky, geometric look, and he often hung cords and tassels form the extended uprights, At the 1902 Turin Exhibition in Italy the wood of some of his furniture was completely covered in vellum, and sporadically decorated with abstract and naturalistic designs such as insects and bird.

HARRY BERTOIA

Born in northern Italy in 1915, Bertoia grew up surrounded by chairs of the Milan School, which greatly influenced his later work. Having emigrated to the United States, he became a metalworker and a student sculptor. He met Eero Saarinen and worked for some years with Charles Eames.

His most famous design is the wire-grid backed dining chair, which became a lasting image of the 1960s, and was described by Bertoia as being 'mainly made of air, like sculpture. Space passes through them'.

SOFAS

The same division between designer-made and mass-produced piece exists in sofa design; but it is the industrialisation of design, which has remained the predominant force in popular sofa design of this century. Despite the speed of change there is a parallel with the development of sofas in the 1800s, when simplicity characterised fashionable pieces in the early years, to be followed by a passion for new materials and methods that were forgotten by the end of the century, when more ornamental seat furniture, often in antique styles became fashionable.

Alongside early twentieth century designer furniture which attracted only a small segment of the market, were the many reproductions of eighteenth century designs, some of which

Below: The Transat chair by Eileen Gray, c. 1927. This elegantly simple chair is punctuated with Germanic brass fittings, has a French look and yet leans towards Mies van der Rohe.

Above: An American interior containing an upholstered wood sofa, c. 1940s. American designers led the world in the 1940s, as war in Europe restricted furniture making to the most economical styles. The sofa is composed of rectangular shapes that were later to form the basis of many mass-produced pieces in the 1970s; it is upholstered in a blue-green textured fabric. At the fireplace side there is only a soft cushion, but the other arm is upholstered over wood to form a support for the integral shelves that act as an occasional table.

Right: An English Arts and Crafts Living Room with built-in sofa designed by M Baillie Scott, 1911. This represents a lighter interpretation of the Art and Crafts tradition. Baillie Scott favoured painted interiors combining furniture and wall decoration to give a somewhat medieval atmosphere.

where made to such high standards that they now command a good price. Favourites were sofas with loose chintzy covers, a type that was especially popular for use in the fashionable cottage-style houses that were built in the suburbs as well as in the country. Because of its adaptability, chintz-covered seat furniture has never gone completely out of fashion.

World War I inhibited the development of European furniture designs, but across the Atlantic styles were much livelier. There was a vogue for pale silk-upholstered sofas in plain, rather square designs, a perfect complement for the cigarette-smoking, gramophone-playing flappers of the early 1920s. Europe caught up with American ideas in the 1930s, and strident colours such as green and red or orange and black were used for the upholstery. Geometric appliqué tassels and various metallic effects were also applied in the Jazz Age, when sofas became the centre of a new extravagant lifestyle. Animal-skin covers gave a striking primitive look to a new metal-framed sofas, while velvet was printed in zebra or leopard patterns.

The most expensive sofas today have feather-filled cushions and sprung constructions. Synthetic upholstery fabrics, plastic re-formed cushions and laminated woods are now mainly reserved for cheap mass-production sofas. The transition from button-backed sofas with turned legs found in every parlour before Word War I, to the Space Age attenuated steel or chrome sculptural works of the 1950s and 1960s, is a reflection of the radical changes and advances in manufacturing methods.

Today, we have true mass-production with pre-formed foam padding and simple upholstery that is frequently fixed in place with metal staples. While such production methods have meant that comfortable seating is available to people of all income levels, craftsmanship and the quality of design have suffered, often resulting in dull uniformity. A few exclusive firms produce finer work, but they often concentrate on traditional styles of reproduction, with exciting sofas appearing only in

Scott to supply fashionable people with well made furniture that looked effective in the new-style interiors from which Victorian clutter was banished. Upholstery colour,s again in reaction to the dark richness of Victorian rooms, was much lighter, their patterns simpler. Pale greens, cool pinks and fresh lilacs formed a good background for furniture in the high-backed idiom of Charles Rennie Mackintosh, or the sinuous curves of the Art Nouveau

The last quarter of this century has seen great contrasts of style, ranging from the sculptural construction of artist-craftsmen, to the traditionally-styled sofa that belongs to no particular period. Many of the best designs are directed at the office and contract furnishing trades.

SOFT FURNISHINGS

Art Deco designers often paid homage to the heritage of Louis XV and Louis XVI and the Empire periods, as well as creating entirely new forms of their own. They used both innovative and traditional materials, although their techniques were usually subsidiary to the overall aesthetic affect. Colours were often bright and vibrant, but subtler pastel shades,

Left: An Italian Art Nouveau Banquette by Carlo Bugatti c. 1900. Part of a wonderful drawing room suite, this is one of the most arresting sofas ever designed. It combines metallic insets with light and dark woods in a curious Italian interpretation of the Art Nouveau style.

Top: An English cretonne-covered Chesterfield sofa, 1920s. In the 1920s ordinary working people were able to buy new furniture for their homes. As many had small sitting rooms, traditional designs, such as the Chesterfield were adapted for such interiors. Deep-padded and well sprung, it is extremely comfortable. The basic version was sold covered in plain cotton upholstery.

(mostly trade) exhibitions or in the design studios of a few innovative craftsmen.

The most desirable sofas are made by well-known progressive designers whose work sets trends that were often modified for the popular market. In the early years of the century, British firms like Heal & Son in London worked very much in the traditions of C.F. A. Voysey and Mackay Hugh Baillie

Right: An American 'soft pad sofa' by Charles Eames, 1982. Many modern sofa designs look as good in a business environment as they do in a domestic one. Designed in 1978 but not made until 1982, this was Charles Eames' last design. It is structured to give maximum support to the shoulders and head.

and deep, dark grays and browns and blacks were also in evidence. The high style Art Deco interiors and furnishings in Paris were, above all, luxurious and lavish, and wealthy clients such as the couturiers Jacques Doucet, Jeanne Lanvin and Madeleine Vionnet, commissioned furniture, objets and even whole rooms. By the late 1930s, upholstery colours had also become simpler, with creams and brown shades predominating, although abstract patterns, especially wavy lines and triangles, often cut moquette, were very popular.

Above: English painted and upholstered sofa by Duncan Grant and Vanessa Bell, mid-1930s. Custom designed, the fabric for the sofa was specially printed to complement the murals and the setting, where furniture was not intended to intrude, but to form part of a complete harmony. This simple upholstered sofa demonstrates the very different approach of the artistic avant-garde in the 1930s and 1940s in comparison to the austere work of the leading German designers who were banishing all superfluous decoration from their creations

Right: A French Art Deco lacquered chaise longue by Pierre Legrain c. 1925. The 'zebra skin' is in fact made from printed velvet, and the armrest, usually against a wall and therefore invisible, is beautifully decorated with mother-of-pearl. Although its structures looks very simple, almost crude, the sofa is beautifully finished, making it an exotic and expansive fancy.

TABLES

Since 1900, explosive changes in fashion and art have produced a wide and confusing range of tables, varying from revived antique styles in the Chippendale vein, to modernist towers of plate glass. A simple way of placing a table within a sensible context is by asking the questions: 'Is this table made up mostly of clean, straight lines, or is it curved and decorated with rich patterns, exotic wood grain and carving?' These two types of tables swing in and out of favour over the first half go the century and indeed afterwards. Twentieth century tables have been designed in a wide variety of new materials such as plastics, plywood and tubular metal, with designers vying with each other to produce innovative, often unconventional shapes.

EARLY TWENTIETH CENTURY TABLES

The Arts and Crafts firms of the nineteenth century influenced the straight, clean lines of table makers of the early twentieth century. These included Charles Rennie Mackintosh's tables with plain lacquer or painted finishes, a minimum of decoration, and often of a rather grand size. Frank Lloyd Wright in America, and Josef Hoffmann in Vienna, with his colleague Koloman Moser, produced designer tables of black and white metal grids during the first 20 years of the century. The students from that workshop carried the 'gospel' of the straight line all over Europe.

CHARLES RENNIE MACKINTOSH

The designs of Scots architect Charles Rennie Mackintosh (1868–1928) show a breathtaking virtuosity – even if they are sometimes self-indulgent. It is easy to understand why his furniture was not well received in Britain: simplicity was sacrificed to sophistication, tradition was flouted, and scant respect was shown for materials. The furniture was made from various woods such as oak, cypress, pine and mahogany, which were rarely left untreated, being either French polished, stained, ebonised, or painted. Among his sources were the massive forms associated with the Scottish baronial tradition. His simple, undecorated designs also show a Japanese influence. Any decoration was restrained, often simply cut-out as seen on the cupboards on the walls in his rooms.

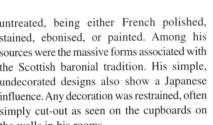

Previous page: A Scottish white panel table by Charles Rennie Mackintosh, c. 1900. This table is one of Mackintosh's more friendly domestic pieces The enamel-like surface was obtained by a coach painting technique which was very smooth and similar to lacquer. This example has an enamel glass inset to contrast with the large flat surface. The table's legs broaden toward the floor, a form emphasising the vertical lines and complementing the elliptical shape of the top.

Below: *An Italian card table by Carlo Graffi, c. 1950. The influence of the Milan School, particularly its premier exponent, Carlo Mollino, is clear in Graffi's juxtaposition of materials, in this case wood and glass on a card table. The wood is unconventionally cut into a shape, which is not inherently strong, but is stressed by tensioning bars, a technique used extensively by Mollino in the 1940s and 1950s. There are also similarities to eighteenth century neo-classical card tables: it is stylish with straight legs and a severe outline, and trays for the counters slide out from each corner, just as candlestick holder slid out from beneath such tables in the 1700s.*

Mackintosh's concern with minimal decoration and curve was in fact one of the main forces behind the conversion to line rather than form, an idea that was expanded by Josef Hoffmann and others in Vienna, and Frank Lloyd Wright in the United States. Mackintosh was primarily an architect, and his limited output of building show his progression from the organic forms associated with Art Nouveau to the linear geometric forms of proto-modernism.

Many of Mackintosh's designs were paro-

Below: Scottish furniture by Charles Rennie Mackintosh, c. 1900. This ebonised table is based on medieval principles: it is heavily built, plain timbered, and virtually undecorated. It is arched between the legs and is very dignified and monumental.

Below: Asprey dining table, c. 1925. Commissioned by an Indian maharajah from Asprey of Bond Street, the table is inlaid with panels from René Lalique of France. Combining these delicate panels, depicting birds among foliage, with heavy square section legs has a monumentally impressive effect.

dies of traditional styles of furniture, His ladder-back chairs, for example, had an exaggeratedly high back with it narrow uprights ridiculously close together, and his table s were often monumental and lacking decoration. His belief was that furniture should fit its settings.

In the early years of the century, several British firms made furniture heavily influenced by Mackintosh and other Arts and Crafts designers. Liberty & Co.. made stained oak furniture often decorated with repoussé copper panels and fruitwood, metal, and mother-of-pearl inlay. Another firm, Wylie & Lochhead of Glasgow, produced furniture in a style that can only be called idiosyncratic. Like Liberty's furniture, it was often elaborately inlaid, and the wood was often stained unusual colours such as grey or violet.

John Sollie Henry's firm in London made similar furniture. Henry himself did much of the designing, favouring mahogany as a material. However, he also commissioned designs from C.F.A. Voysey, W.A.S. Benson and George Walton. Several of his pieces were designed by George Monatgue Ellwood (1875–c.1960).

Other influential designers included Edwin Lutyens and Gerald Summers, who designed pieces of innovative furniture for the firm Makers of Simple Furniture. Lloyd Loom furniture achieved popular status, and some glass and chrome dining furniture, illuminated and inlaid with panels from Lalique was produce by Asprey.

FRENCH ART NOUVEAU

The other branch of Art Nouveau was French in origin. There were two design centres one in Paris, the other in Nancy, where Emile Gallé (1846–1904) produced handsome tables, chairs, and case pieces with sensuous curves and ornate-inspired embellishments. Gallé was a prominent founding member of the Nancy School of Art Nouveau design, based in Lorraine. Most of his output was glass and ceramic: his cameo-glass vases and relief

designs are probably his best work. Gallé produced furniture from the mid-1880s onward, inspired in part by his visit to a stockist of exotic woods. He felt that Art Nouveau motifs should be applied to conventional construction, believing that individuality lay in ornamentation. Hence, he used blank surfaces for his subtle decoration. The flat tops of his tables were irregular shapes often inlaid with landscapes, blossoms, and twisting stems; their legs likewise were rarely straight, but instead were carved, in some cases like spreading vines, in others as massive dragonflies.

Parisian Hector Guimard (best known for designing the metalwork entrances to Parisian métro stations) designed tables with amazing undulating curves. These were very much akin to his magnificent ornate wrought iron designs.

Antoni Gaudi of Barcelona, whose amorphic shapes feature knobbly knees and crooked elbows, sometimes with wrought iron supports, used similar features in his designs too. The distinction between tables with straight lines and those with curves and decoration adapted from nature extended into the Art Deco period, although the later elements become much more stylised and less organic in the 1920s

FRENCH ART DECO

One of the most famous ébénistes of Art Deco France was Emile-Jacques Ruhlmann (1879–1933). After tentatively exhibiting his work before World War I, he came to dominate French interior design in the 1920s. His furniture is often compared to the work of great eighteenth century French cabinet-makers. Of excellent quality and made at great expense, Ruhlmann use exotic hardwoods such as ebony, and used ivory and shagreen (sharkskin) for detail. He frequently used exotic

fabrics such as leopardskin with coloured woods and lacquering. His trademark was the brass sabots (literally clogs) which echoed the mounts of eighteenth century tables. Ruhlmann was supported through much of his working life by wealthy patrons. He stated that the proportions of his furniture as a whole were far more important than their detail or ornamentation, but the luxury and style of his work – especially the applied decoration – are

Below: A French Art Deco dressing table by Emile-Jacques Ruhlmann, 1925. This piece came from the peak of Ruhlmann's neo-classical phase. It has tapering legs and brass-capped sabots.

Below: The end table by Gerrit Rietveld, originally designed in 1923. This table is a replica and shows the influence of the Dutch De Stijl movement which reduced objects to simple geometric and linear elements, and used the primary colours of red, yellow and blue as a contrast to the non-colours of black white and grey.

Main picture: A set of chairs and a games table by Emile-Jacques Ruhlmann, c. 1920. The tapering legs and brass sabots, Ruhlmann's trademarks are clearly visible in these items. Uncharacteristically, the upholstery is restrained.

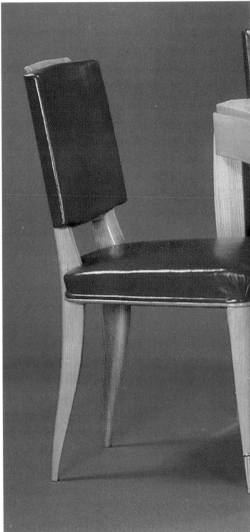

outstanding. His devotion to the excess and virtues of éitism could not have been further from the ideals of the English Arts and Crafts Movement or the soon-to-dominate German Bauhaus.

ARMAND-ALBERT RATEAU

The expression of Art Deco style in France was most obvious in the Parisians interiors of the 1920s and 1930s. In 1920, for example, Jeanne Lanvin commissioned Armand-Albert Rateau (1882–1938) to design the interior of her Paris house. His patinated bronze, wood ,and marble furnishings abounded with elaborate floral and animals motifs – birds supporting a bronze coffee table, deer and foliage on the bathroom bas relief, marguerites entwining a dressing table, and fire-dogs in the shape of cats. Rateau's furniture and overall vision are among the most figurative and truly sculptural of the period. However, the heavily veneered, embellished or often lacquered pieces of many of his contemporaries are more handsome and restrained, often deriving from such classical shapes as scrolls, and using stylised forms for animals, wings, birds, and human figures.

Left: A French Art Deco bronze and marble table by Armand-Albert Rateau, c. 1925. This example has a marble top in the form of a large tray, reminiscent of ancient Chinese ceremonial vessels. Its legs are stylised forms of a bird, perhaps a peacock, and they have an archaic feel to them. Rateau was directly influenced by the classical Roman furniture in metal he viewed on a visit to Herculaneum and Pompeii.

Below: Austrian tables by Josef Hoffmann 1901–1910.
[A] This pedestal table adapts traditional forms with straight lines and new materials, smooth surfaces of stained wood and metal details for effect and strength.
[B] Designed for Kabarett Fledermaus, for a theatre-bar in Vienna, this is a strongly geometric table, with typically smooth surfaces and restrained colour.
[C] This model retains the straight lines and is a classic geometric design that is still made today by the German firm Franz Wittmann which reproduces several other chairs and tables by Hoffmann.

DE STIJL MOVEMENT

In 1915 in the Netherlands the De Stijl movement applied the affection for rectilinearity, primary colours and flat surfaces to furniture making, A carpenter by training, Gerrit Rietveld made geometric- shaped tables which even today seem revolutionary. In 1923 he designed his End table, which was produced by G.A van de Groenekan who worked with Rietveld throughout his life on some of his most ambitious and bizarre compositions. Intended for the Schroeder House in Utrecht as part of an overall scheme based on basic architectural principles, it was later joined by his Berlin chair.

AUSTRIAN TABLES

Josef Hoffmann, a founder member of the Wiener Werkstätte, was another exponent of the geometric, linear branch of Art Nouveau expression. His designs concentrate on contrasting colours, straight lines, and the formation of grids to define space. He was much inspired by Charles Rennie Mackintosh. The Wiener Werkstätte were set up to manufacture the new design styles in Vienna and the enterprise proved enormously successful over several decades, producing mainly expensive furniture for an élite clientele.

Around 1900 the beginning of Hoffmann's move away from conventional rectilinear furni-

B

A

C

ture were seen in the interiors of houses he designed, such as the Palais Stoclet in Brussels. The new style of furniture was also shown at the Paris Exhibitions, which were influential platforms for innovative ideas. Hoffmann designed several tables but as he became better known his commissions varied greatly.

The Viennese architect Adolf Loos (1870-1933) was also influenced by British crafts-manship, particularly the Arts and Crafts Movement. He produced an intriguing table made from walnut and copper. Familiarly known as the 'Elephant table', or the 'Spider table', it is circular, with each of its eight cabriole legs supported on a semi-circle. It is not functional, but it has an interesting shape inspired by geometry and oriental influences.

ALVAR AALTO AND THE BAUHAUS

In Germany Bauhaus students concentrated on new materials and techniques, creating machine age tables of tubular steel with glass and often no decoration save a chrome finish. In Finland Alvar Aalto experimented with novel uses for plywood. They perfected these materials with new woods and glues, producing moulded tables and trolleys from one or very few parts. Crucial advances were being made using a variety of new materials and methods, and the increasing use of plastics also led to a preponderance of synthetic tables. Aalto was a talented and prodigious architect-designer. He was responsible for over 200 buildings, concerning himself with lighting, heating, acoustics and exterior surroundings, as well as furniture as an accessory to architecture.

Below: Scandinavian plywood table by Alvar Aalto, c. 1931. One of Aalto's major projects was the Paimio Sanatorium in Finland in the 1930s. This table was designed in conjunction with Aalto's wife, Aino Marsio, as part of an experimental design portfolio for much of the hospital.

Below left: A tea trolley by Alvar Aalto c. 1937. This tea trolley developed from the 'dumb waiter', a three-tiered table on castors which could be placed or wheeled near to the main dining table. This trolley shows a freshness of design and lack of decoration; it is at once attractive and functional.

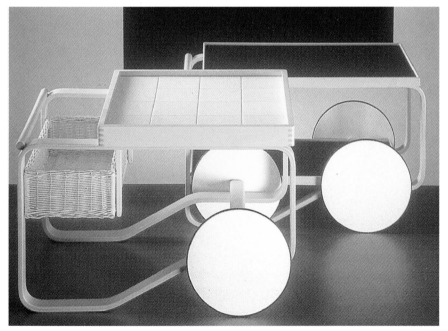

Below: A French wrought iron console table by Raymond Subes, c. 1935. The breakfront table with black marble top (its centre section set slightly forward) echoes the Georgian bookcases of the eighteenth century.

He believed that the human form should only touch natural materials. Wood is good acoustically as it absorbs sound, and Aalto's belief that it was pliable enough not to be cut or carved led to the development of his bent laminate plywood pieces.

RAYMOND SUBES

Raymond Subes, (1893–1970) who was born in Paris, studied metal engraving at Ecole Boulle, the Parisian school of metalwork, before working for the influential architects Borderel and Robert. In 1919, he became the director of their metal workshop and he was responsible for many important architectural projects, He usually worked in wrought iron,

but also used bronze copper and aluminium. Subes's work followed on from the revival of metalwork as an Arts and Crafts interest in the nineteenth century, and of the great Art Deco metalworker, Edgar Brandt (1880–1960). Brandt and Subes both worked for the top designers of the time and exhibited under their own names.

DECORATION

During the Art Deco era, designers turned to rich materials both traditional and exotic including lacquer, snakeskin, marble, and sharkskin., Jacques Henri Lartigue, for example, supported a table on a striking sphere of marble, and Rose Adler inlaid a black

lacquer tables with coquille d'oeuf (crushed eggshell, an oriental innovation). Typical Parisian furniture tended to used conventional materials and be based on styles ranging from Louis XV to tribal African, but there was still competition in the form of tubular metal.

Lartigue was also known for his writing and photography, as well as his furniture design and he is associated with the Modern Movement which stressed function and utility as opposed to the sumptuous and luxurious excess of the Art Deco style. Le Corbusier's phrase that, 'houses are machines for living in' came to epitomise such ideals.

The designer largely responsibly for the revival of sharkskin as a veneering material is generally reckoned to be Clément Rousseau. 'Shagreen', as it is known, was used in conjunction with a variety of woods, to particular dramatic effect on table tops, and could be tinted in a variety of colours. Rousseau was patronised by the couturier Jacques Doucet, and several of his pieces can be found at Doucet's villa at Neuilly.

ITALIAN DESIGN EXPRESSION

Machine-age furniture and popular antique reproduction styles co.-existed in Italian table design. In the postwar period, Milan took on increasing importance as designers such as Carlo Mollino (1905–1973) produced light-hearted economical tables, The use of plywood increased, and it was often combined with other materials such as formica (a laminated plastic). The Milan designers developed an optimistic style whose tables feature light construction and bright colours. Throughout the 1960s and up to the present day Italy has produced not only functional, but also visually exciting designs.

Below left: A reproduction of a table by Jacques-Henri Lartigue originally designed 1918. This is a remake of the classic table by Lartigue which was originally made of ivory and black-lacquered wood in 1918 and now reproduced by French designer-manufacture Ecart. Lartigue successfully combined geometric shapes and exotic materials, in typical Art Deco style, with the Modernist notion of structural simplicity. The bold, original sculpture feels quite at home in the 1980s.

Below: A sharkskin and ebony table, c. 1930. Probably made by Clément Rousseau, this table is made of tinted sharkskin and ebony, and has a sunburst motif on the flat surface. The table bears a striking resemblance to a chair made by Rousseau about 1921.

Below right: Oak dining suite by Gordon Russell, c. 1950. The design for the suite is retrospective. Russell became a specialist in industrial production, and during World War II designed British utility furniture, which concentrated scarce resources on making only one type of furniture as cheaply as possible.

Below: A trapezoidal Harpies coffee table by Alberto Giacometti, c. 1955. This table comes from a series of bronze and glass furniture based on skeletal human and organic forms. Here the form of the harpy – a mythical monster with a woman's head and body and limbs of a bird – is used as the decoration on the twig-like legs and stretcher. The whole piece is cast in bronze.

The influence of the Milan School, particularly its premier exponent, the innovative designer Carlo Mollino, can be seen in the stylish work of Carlo Graffi, especially his juxtaposition of materials, such as wood and glass.

ALBERTO GIACOMETTI.

Alberto Giacometti (1901–66) was a Swiss-born sculptor, painter and poet, who trained in Italy in the 1920s, While he was there he was greatly influenced by the Romanian-born sculptor Constantin Brancusi (1876–1957). In the 1930s Giacometti produced mainly surreal works with mythological and mysterious elements, and he later went on to concentrate on the stick –like emaciated figures, made from wire frames, applied with plaster of Paris for which he is perhaps best known. His furniture is generally fairly light-hearted and its highly prized by collectors of twentieth

century works. His tables are often a combination of glass and his trademark intricate, spindly metalwork, based on human or organic forms.

AMERICAN EXPRESSIONS

With their built-in strength, plastic and fibreglass allowed the new furniture shapes to be moulded. Charles Eames, one of the most influential American furniture designers of the century, experimented with plywood during World War II, and afterwards produced a monochromatic, single pedestal table, all made

of glass reinforced with polyester – a truly novel creation.

A long time collaborator of Charles Eames was Eero Saarinen. Finish-born Saarinen was the son of the designer Eliel Saarinen. After studying sculpture in Paris, he graduated from the Yale School of Architecture. Despite his American nationality, his furniture still shows an element of Scandinavian elegance and a desire for simplicity. He once declared that 'the underside of typical chairs and tables makes a confusing, unrestful world. I want to clear up the slum of legs'.

BRITISH STYLE

Great Britain also produced good quality tables, especially some in the no-frills traditional vein such as those by Gordon Russell, (1892–1980) whose sturdy forms looked back to the nineteenth century Arts and Crafts furniture. In the 1980s the Gordon Russell Design Group produced modular sofa groups which have since become popular in office reception areas or to form a rectangular seating area around a fire in the domestic setting. The emphasis of their designs is comfort, but the good basic design shape is an attractive alter-

Below: Pedestal tables by Eero Saarinen, c. 1955. Tables supported by a single pedestal reached their peak of popularity in the nineteenth century. However, the weakness of wooden joints generally led to stocky pedestals. Here, Saarinen uses modern materials to produce a more elegant range of chairs and tables

Below: The Green Table by Allen Jones, c. 1972. One of a limited edition of six, the table is constructed from glass fibre, leather and other accessories. This table offers a curious twist to the traditional use of the human figure to support tables and other furniture, a device common in the seventeenth and eighteenth centuries.

native to the many bland items found in the local furniture shop.

The Swinging Sixties, on the other hand, gave birth to bizarre Pop Art such as Allen Jones' Tables Sculpture, whose base is a crouching, sadomasochistic woman; this is a good example of how new materials (painted glassfibre and resin) allowed the return of tables based on shapes and curves. Some of his designs are deliberately provocative, and while having little place in history as functional items, his table carries on the precedent of fantasy furniture as seen in the eighteenth century Rococo and earlier Baroque work ,as well as the twentieth century designs of Salvador Dali.

HABITAT FORMING

The first Habitat catalogue appeared in 1971. It combined Habitat-designed wares with the work of other designers, including Eero Saarinen and Harry Bertoia. Mass production kept prices down, and the imaginative room settings in the catalogue promoted the idea of more stylish households. Easy access by post, or by visiting the rapidly growing chain of stores ensured Habitat's success. There is, in fact ,little in the first catalogue of tremendous originality. It focused on the practical, clean lines of the 1960s, with bright colours and some up-market furniture including the founder, Terence Conran's own design line.

The Habitat range created a means for bour-

geois style that it then exploited with a chain of stores that were somehow very different from the traditional British quality stores, such as Heals.

DANNY LANE

In the 1980s there were two main design streams for tables. Functional tables made for use, such as may be bought in any large store and are relatively inexpensive to make, utilising new materials and methods; and tables made for arts' sake. Danny Lane's creations are the latter. Made from stacks of glass, they are not intended to be functional, but are entirely sculptural.

Danny Lane has already been acclaimed as a producer of classic design. An American who has lived and worked in London since the 1970s, Lane subverts the conventional notion of how glass should be used. His glass furniture is certainly dramatic and contains the sort of glistening apparitions which the seventeenth and eighteenth centuries would have greatly appreciated. Glass chairs are extremely rare, although some were produced in the nineteenth century in formal throne-like precisely cut material. Danny Lane uses dozens of individual slices of float glass which are held together by rods in columns. His furniture is amusing and exciting, epithets which could equally have been applied to Rococo or more bizarre Regency designs.

Below: The first Habitat range of furniture, c. 1971 Taken from the first Habitat catalogue, the items in this photograph show clean lines and bright colours, in modern materials.

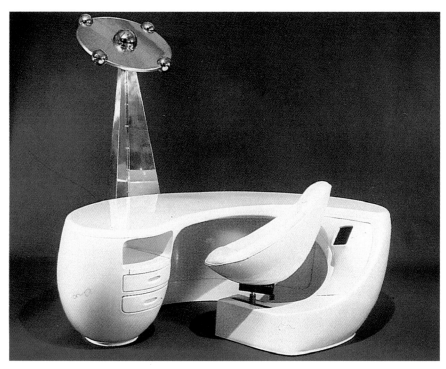

1980s STYLE

As in previous centuries, designers from the twentieth century have drawn their inspiration from earlier styles. In the last quarter of the twentieth century several designers revisited Art Deco and Bauhaus styles.

André Putman, a Parisian interior designer has many of his pieces produced by Ecart International. A lot of his work has an Art Deco flavour about it, although it is obviously modern.

Ettore Sottsass took part in producing some designs in the 1980s heavily influenced by Bauhaus design. Sottsass was born in 1917 in Austria and has worked with bodies as diverse as Olivetti and the Royal College of Art. He was also one of the organisers of the radical Memphis Collection, an exhibition in Milan in 1981. He describes himself as 'a metamorphic designer', and considers the object itself to be relatively unimportant: rather he is more concerned with how it is represented. This he achieves by using bright colours and unusual shapes. His furniture, such as the Spyder table, for example, is said to show a sense of irony and wit, and often refers to animal or human form.

Below: Solomon's table by Danny Lane, c. 1988. Table or sculpture? Made of marble and glass, this table resembles a surfboard or a fish suspended by towering plates of cut glass. Glass construction is a trademark of Danny Lane's (b.1955) an Illinois native who now lives in London and ranks among the most successful of modern designers.

Lane claims that his pieces evolve naturally out to the medium he is using. This bold design utilises light and colour to show the materials to good effect; very much the same principles in fact that designers of all periods have employed in furniture making over the centuries.

DESKS AND CABINETS

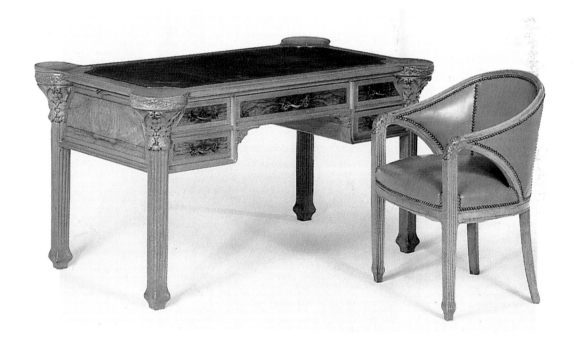

During the twentieth century desks and cabinets have been produced in a variety of styles. Traditional designs that are a homage to the elegant pieces of eighteenth century cabinet-makers remain popular today. Contemporary designs, produced in metal, fibreglass or plastic provide a dramatic contrast to such classic items. It was the new man-made materials that enabled Modernist designers like Frank Lloyd Wright to make the dramatic leap in thinking that allowed them to produce pieces completely free of classical restraint, uninfluenced by decorative styles of the past. In essence, however, an eclectic variety of desks and cabinets have existed side-by-side throughout the century.

DESIGN FIT FOR PURPOSE

Throughout the century writing desks have continued to be made in antiques styles. Such imitations can be seen as an endorsement of the functional designs of earlier craftsmen, but it is also a reflection on the status of the writing desk as an accepted, even though increasingly old-fashioned, item of furniture. In the early part of the nineteenth century furniture was embellished and sometimes even completely covered. Throughout the twentieth century shapes of furniture have ranged from the overtly traditional – eighteenth century bureau plats, ladies desks or bérgère chairs, for example – to strikingly modern, severe recti-linear styles, with not a curve in sight. It is the novelties of an age – radios and refriger-ators being twentieth century examples – that tend to attract the most distinctive and progressive styling. In terms of the evolution of desks, however, it was not the home that was most affected, but the office, itself an increasingly important arena of modern life, which has been further complicated by the advent of modern office paraphernalia.

In the twentieth century the flat-topped library table is the general model for the office desk. In the office, other technological advances like the typewriter and the telephone have tended to dictate the need for simple flat surfaces with drawers beneath, especially as this form was well suited to the trend towards clean, efficient design. Faced with a welter of cables and the loom of the visual display unit, the traditional desk has retreated – but only as far as the offices of senior management, where a large imposing antique desk has always added respectability to power. It is inter-esting to note, however, that a variety of

Below: A fibreglass desk and chair by Jean Leleu, c. 1969. Although this looks dated now, it was extremely outrageous at the time, and in fact represents a union of three distinct trends. First, it owes a debt of origin to Charles Eames, Eero Saarinen and even Harry Bertioia, who exploited and explored the use of new materials in a soft sculptural way. Second, it fully exploits the possibility of fibreglass, its great strength and ease of construction creates an integral sculptural environment for the user. This idea was not a novelty – many people have sat at a Victorian desk with a folding bench seat – but what is new is the harmony of line in this extravagance. Third it marks the outer boundary of the avant-garde as allowed by the new materials (just as it could be said that the English Habitat designs of moulded fibre furniture were the inner boundary). A brief look at the 1980s shows regression from this degree of innovation or at least a return to more traditional forms.

traditional desks are now produced with cunning shelves and apertures designed to accommodate computer paraphernalia, producing a rather uneasy marriage between the elegant writing surfaces of the past, and the screens, keyboards and cables so vital to the E-mail generation.

EARLY TWENTIETH CENTURY DESIGN STYLES

At the beginning of this century, the writing desk, now an essential part of the well-equipped middle-class home, was found in many different guises, but the well-tried solutions of the past – fall-fronts, fitted drawers and pull-out slides – were generally retained even when the overall style was avant-garde. Art Nouveau was one of the most widely disseminated of the international styles, and it continued to exert an influence in the first decade of the century. It had emerged in continental Europe in the 1880s as a conscious

attempt to create something new to replace the worn-out revivals that dominated the salon furniture of the time. In France, after the Paris Exposition of 1900, a reaction set in and several designers started working in a much more restrained manner, drawing their inspiration from eighteenth century neo-classicism and French country design.

THE WORK OF VICTOR HORTA

The Belgian architect Victor Horta (1861-1947) created flamboyant Art Nouveau furniture for his interiors. Characterised by whiplash curves, scrolling curved ironwork and stained glass, Horta revealed his debt to the Rococo forms of the eighteenth century. He produced a particularly fine wooden buffet in 1900 for his own home whose angularity was offset by curving scrollwork around the doors and elaborate metal handles and hinges.

By 1905, Horta had exhausted his Art

Below: An Italian office desk of tubular and sheet steel, vinyl and cloth. This whole concept is made up from modules of the Spazio system launched by Olivetti in 1961. Olivetti produced a series of standard modules that could be manufactured cheaply and which could be made up by the customer to fit any office. This is an early and stylish example of the trend towards factory-produced DIY furniture.

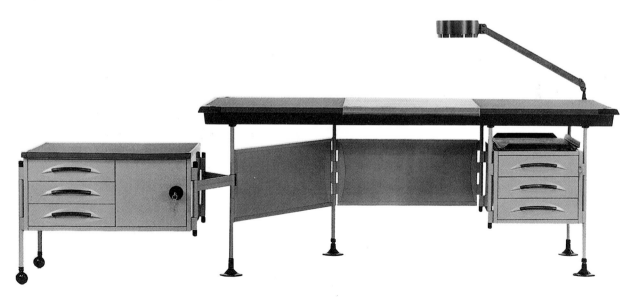

Below: A Scottish ebonised oak mother-of-pearl, metal and glass writing cabinet, 1904. This writing cabinet, 3ft wide, was made for the study of the Scottish architect Charles Rennie Mackintosh to his own design. Here, the desk is shown open to reveal pigeonholes and shelves over the writing surface, with an open folio stand below. The stark, angular design, relieved by the sparkle of the small pieces of glass and mother-of-pearl, is typical of Mackintosh's work, as is the distinctive glass and metal flower panel at the centre of the cabinet.

Nouveau creativity, turning instead to abstract forms derived from nature. He created the idea of built-in furniture which became typical of the Art Nouveau interior. The French writer Edmond Goncourt referred to it as 'yachting style': a banquette would run along one wall, turn a corner and finish as a display case.

LOUIS MAJORELLE AND THE NANCY SCHOOL
Louis Majorelle (1859–1926) was a prominent member of the Nancy School of design, a group of French architects and designers who promoted 'organic' Art Nouveau. Emile Gallé, famous for his glassware and ceramics was active in founding the school, which is closely associated with the area around Nancy in north-eastern France.

Majorelle originally trained as a painter before taking over his father's furniture

factory in the late 1870s. His speciality was sophisticated furniture such as that designed for upmarket Paris restaurants like *Chez Maxim*, and although his early furniture was traditional he was quick to adopt the nature-inspired forms of Art Nouveau. Much of his work is in fairly dark, hard woods such as mahogany or walnut, with decoration on the upholstery or the sides of drawers and tables.

EUROPEAN DESIGNERS
In Europe between the wars, one of the leading influences on functional design was the Bauhaus, which established design standards that were adapted to machine production and spawned a generation of obviously modern utilitarian furniture.

Germany suffered economically under the harsh conditions laid down by the Treaty of

Versailles (1919) which led to the financial collapse of 1926 and the depression of the 1930s. But good cheap design did not have to be a luxury, and until 1933 it would be true to say that France's position at the centre of the art world was challenged by Germany.

CHARLES RENNIE MACKINTOSH

The designs of Scots architect Charles Rennie Mackintosh (1868–1928) show a breath-taking virtuosity – even if they are sometimes self-indulgent.

One of Mackintosh's most important

Below: An English writing cabinet, veneered in ebony and holly. This beautiful piece of furniture, with decorative painting and fittings, and mounts of wrought iron and silver, was designed by Charles Robert Ashbee in 1902.

Below: An Art Deco partner's desk and chair c. 1915. This functional writing desk and chair show how stylish Art Deco features could be incorporated into practical design. Although luxurious and high-quality work, the table's use of fruit-wood veneer is not unusual, its tapering legs are not excessive and the repeated coil decoration is minimal. It is probably the work of Pail Iribe

Below right: French black lacquer Art Deco kneehole desk and chair. This desk was designed by Jean Dunand and Serge Revinski and is 3ft 11in wide with four drawers in each pedestal. The hinged central writing slope is covered with, lozenges of shagreen and the top of each pedestal is hinged to give access to a compartment beneath.

commissions was the desk designed for Hill House, the home of Glasgow publisher Walter Blackie. His highly individual furniture forms were both influenced by and reacted against the products of the Arts and Crafts Movement, although they were generally more influential on the continent and in America than in Britain.

Charles Robert Ashbee was another leading figure of the British Arts and Crafts Movement in the late nineteenth century and a founder of the Guild and School of Handicraft at Toynbee Hall in the East End of London in 1888. Ashbee followed the basic tenets of the movement in encouraging undivided labour, with each craftsman involved with every stage of the production. Like many other pioneers, however, Ashbee found it difficult to compete with commercial firms, and after a move to the Cotswolds in 1902, the venture folded in 1914.

ROGER FRY AND THE OMEGA WORKSHOP
Working from the Omega Workshop, Roger

Fry (1866–1934)was commissioned in 1916 to design the furnishings for an entire apartment for the wife of the Belgian ambassador, Lalla Vandervelde, who liked the distinctive, brightly painted pieces produced by the young artists at the workshop. Among the pieces commissioned was a marquetry desk whose badly fitting drawers and poor quality marquetry typify the workshop's output

Fry had founded Omega partly as a reaction against the serious craft guild mentality of the post-Morris era, and he was more concerned with spontaneity and artistic expression than with craftsmanship and technique. Nevertheless, he provided many keen young artists with a means of earning a living, and by cultivating clients managed to see the workshops through the difficult days of World War I, finally closing in 1921.

ART DECO DESKS
More than any other type of furniture, desk design was improved considerably by the application of the concept of function rather

Right top: A French Art Deco pedestal desk, veneered in rosewood by Jules Leleu, c. 1930. The drawers of the item are in each end of a large pedestal, and on one side of each smaller pedestal. The three-way design is unusual, but the clean, straight lines, the use of rich figured veneer in the wide expanses, and chromium-plated handles and base are typical of the best quality Art Deco furniture.

Left middle: A French half-round pedestal desk. This unusual and attractive piece was a special commission by Jacques-Emile Ruhlmann. The top is fitted with five double-hinged compartments radiating from a leather writing surface with two cut-glass inkwells. The left-hand pedestal is fitted with drawers with gilt bronze handles, and the right-hand with a tambour shutter over a drawer. Both stand on gilt bronze pedestals joined by a gilt bronze stretcher. The distinctive striped veneer is macassar ebony, an exotic wood much favoured by Art Deco furniture designers for its sleek dramatic appearance.

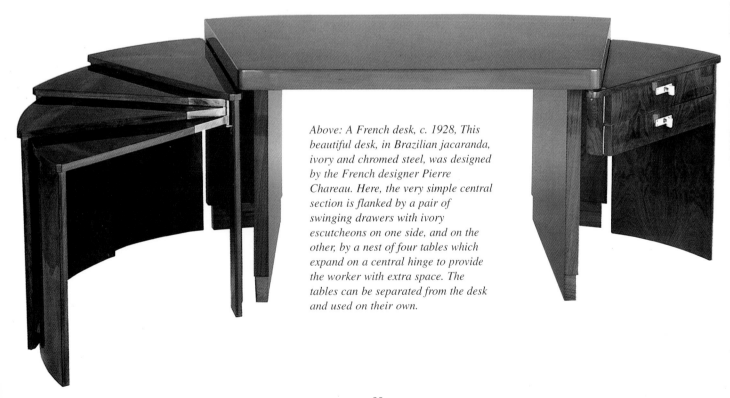

Above: A French desk, c. 1928, This beautiful desk, in Brazilian jacaranda, ivory and chromed steel, was designed by the French designer Pierre Chareau. Here, the very simple central section is flanked by a pair of swinging drawers with ivory escutcheons on one side, and on the other, by a nest of four tables which expand on a central hinge to provide the worker with extra space. The tables can be separated from the desk and used on their own.

Below: An Austrian Secessionist desk, 1902. This piece, designed by the Viennese designer Koloman Moser, is made of elm, ivory, mother-of-pearl, ebony, and jacaranda, and was a special commission for the Château Charlottenlund, near Stockholm. It is shown open for use, and appears sober and symmetrical. However, when the fall-front is lifted and closed it reveals a restrained exoticism typical of the avant-garde Viennese artists of the time. The whole front is inlaid with a parquetry pattern of interlocking squares, and the veneer of the fall-front is decorated with a pair of mother-of-pearl maidens holding inlaid brass rings and flanked by stylised dolphins in ebony.

than form. Nevertheless, the Art Deco period produced many elegant desks that combined utilitarianism with great beauty.

The French architect and interior decorator Pierre Chareau designed luxurious, highly finished interiors, but also gave a great deal of thought to the practical design of desks of all kinds. He favoured combining materials such as jacaranda, ivory and chromed steel, a rich mixture that gave rise to elegant furniture that is highly collectable.

New forms appeared in the years following World War I. The cocktail cabinet, a piece of

furniture unknown until the 1920s, was an innovation of the Jazz Age, answering the need of a generation intent on pleasure after the grim war years. Typically designed with a restrained, sleek look that had already been evident in some of the work of Hoffmann and Moser in Austria, it brought classic Art Deco styles to the notices of a wider public.

Paul Iribe (1883–1935) was noted for the use of coils in his work and was considered one of the more moderate of the avant-garde Art Deco artists. His interesting career included illustrating for various design

magazines; founding the magazine *Le Témoin* (the Witness) in 1905, designing jewellery, fabrics, interiors, and advertisements; and working for Jacques Doucet in his Paris apartment on the Avenue de Bois. Having travelled to the United States in 1914 to work with the film producer-director Cecil B. De Mille, he returned to France in the 1930s and was for sometime associated with Coco Chanel.

Emile-Jacques Ruhlmann is France's best known exponent of Art Deco. His furniture is excellent quality and was made at great expense. Made from a variety of woods with highly decorated motifs and geometric patterns in ebony and ivory, his furniture is widely recognised and admired.

John Dunand (1877–1942) also designed elaborate furniture, including cabinets, panels and screens, which were often covered with figurative or animal designs. While working in Paris he learned the correct oriental technique for lacquering from the Japanese artist Sugawara. The smooth lines and surface on Dunand's furniture designs are the most distinctive of the interwar years.

AUSTRIAN SECESSION
The principal Secession designers were two

Below: A British double architect's desk and matching chair, 1935. This set of painted tubular steel and painted wood was made by the British firm PEL (Practical Equipment Limited). The desk has a single long frieze drawer and three smaller drawers suspended in the framework. It is attached to an adjustable drawing board giving an overall width of nine feet.

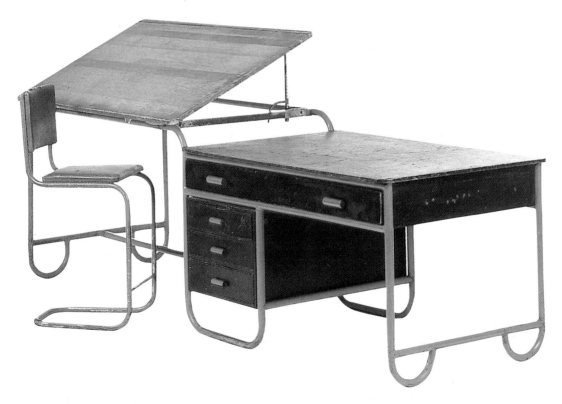

Below: Belgian buffet, wood, c. 1900. Designed by Belgian architect Victor Horta for his own home, the scrolled lines of this piece owe a debt of inspiration to Rococo forms.

young architects Joseph Hoffmann and Koloman Moser who, with a group of artist (including, Otto Wagner, Josef Olbrich and Gustav Klimt) broke away from the conservative Vienna Academy in 1897. Influenced by Mackintosh's work, much of their furniture featured severe rectilinear lines. The Secessionist Exhibition Gallery was opened in 1898 and in 1903 Hoffmann and Moser founded the Wiener Werkstätte (Vienna workshop) which was financed by Waerndorfer and Otto Primavesi. It was a craft co-operative producing metalware, furniture and textiles. Some of the pieces designed by Moser were richly decorated with marquetry or inlaid metals, while others were simply painted white.

Characteristic of Hoffmann's furniture are lattice chair backs and table aprons and small spheres of wood for decoration at points of structural significance. Hoffmann's style gradually became more retrospective, using some neo-classical and Biedermeier forms.

The same influence is evident in the furniture created by Otto Prutscher (880–1949) and Josef Urban (1872–1933), the other Viennese designers. Prutscher also designed for Thonet. Other Viennese manufacturers that employed Wiener Werkstätte designers included Jacob and Joseph Kohn, Portois & Fix, Franz Gloser and Richard Ludwig.

UTILITARIAN BRITAIN

A serious shortage of raw materials during World War II set in its own limitations on furniture design in Britain just as World War I had done, and it led to government intervention in the furniture industry so that only approved designs could be manufactured between 1943 and 1952. The Utility range of furniture that resulted – plain, indecorous, unpretentious, but of a guaranteed minimum quality – was intended to help the refurnishing of bombed out homes, but also helped to establish the idea that utility and good design were not mutually exclusive.

By the mid-1930s British firms were following continental leads in exploiting the strength, economy and clean modern lines of bent tubing. The principle European producer was the Vienna-based firm of Thonet. Having pioneered the mass manufacture of inexpensive bentwood furniture as early as 1830s, they adapted naturally to new materials such as metal tubing and plywood, which had a similar combination of strength and flexibility.

After World War II, plastic became a commonplace material for furniture, and its effects on design have been crucial, moving the emphasis from decoration back to fluidity of line. In Europe, design standards were adapted to machine production and spawned a generation of utilitarian office furniture that was very obviously modern. The need for utilitarian furniture has further increased in the last quarter of the century with the growing importance of computers. Apart from the need to house and use the machines themselves, the new technology has also posed problems in the management of electric cables on a large scale. More recent developments have shown a growing division between pieces of furniture designed and made for the mass market, and items specifically for collectors.

MODERN ITALIAN DESIGN

Italian design received considerable impetus after World War II when so much that had been destroyed needed to be replaced. Designers and artists in the postwar period

Below: An Italian desk with formica top by Carlo Mollino, c. 1955. This pedestal desk is a curious combination of blonde wood and formica. It is typical of Mollino's postwar work when his designs were sculptural and often humorous. The table is more that purely functional; the pedestal placed on one side and the stretchers could have been simpler. The leg construction of this table seems to resemble a bat or an aeroplane.

Below: An Italian oak two-tier desk of the mid-1950s. It is stamped 'Silvio Cavatorta, Roma', but its stylish design clearly shows the influence of the greatest Italian designer of the era, Carlo Mollino. Supported on two K-frames, the top tier serves as a working surface over a shelf, with two added double drawer units below.

were keen to use new materials such as formica, and many of Mollino's earlier designs used the cheaper plywood. His later works echo the stressed plywood construction of his chairs, although he also used solid cut timber for the framework.

Mollino was a prominent member of the Milan School of design which initially gained attention at the first Milan Triennale Exhibition of 1933. His work has often been associated with the architects Franco Albini and Guiseppe Terragni, and the Appelli company of Turin, which has produced much of his work.

AMERICAN DESKS AND CABINETS

Gustav Stickley (1857–1946), editor of the magazine *The Craftsman* from 1901 until 1916, was one of the most practical and successful exponents of the Arts and Crafts ideal in America. Although trained as a stone-

mason, Stickley began working in a relative's chair factory in 1876. He began his career making furniture in a variety of fashionable revival styles, but he took the writings of the Arts and Crafts pioneers to heart and set about producing simple plank-constructed pieces with tenon joints and almost no decoration. He had seen Shaker furniture at the Philadelphia Centennial Exhibition in 1876 and set up his own workshop at Binghampton, New York to make furniture that emulated Shake simplicity. It was not until 1899 when he formed the Gustav Stickley Co. in Eastwood outside Syracuse, New York, that he was able to put his philosophy into practice.

He showed a common sense that many idealists lack, and he was happy to use machines in his workshop where it made the work easier and the product cheaper without interfering with the quality. Stickley's strong sturdy

furniture was made in native hardwoods, often oak, and sometimes inlaid with pewter, iron, or copper, or upholstered in leather or canvas. It was intended to evoke the 'simple life' of the early pioneers. The style soon gained the name 'Missions Furniture', but Stickley wrote in one of his trade catalogues 'I had no idea of attempting to create a new style, but merely tried to make furniture which would be simple, durable, comfortable and fitted for the place it had to occupy and the work it had to do'. In many ways the American public was more

Below: An American oak fall-front desk with iron handles. This is a typical plank-constructed desk, produced by the Stickley Workshop in about 1910.

Below left: An American fall-front desk c. 1904. The panelled fall-front is inlaid with stylised motifs in pewter and various light woods, and conceals an interior with a central drawer surrounded by pigeonholes and shelves. The exterior has been darkened by fuming, a favourite Stickley finish; while the interior is made of much lighter wood. This desk was designed by Harvey Ellis, who worked with Stickley for a period before his death in 1904 and introduced his characteristic inlaid ornament to the company's range.

Left: An American oak, fall-front writing cabinet, c. 1902. This was designed by Frank Lloyd Wright for the house he created for Francis W. Little at Peoria, Illinois. It is 5ft 9in tall, but only 1ft 9in wide and seems to have been intended to stand on one side of the fireplace in the master bedroom, complemented by a similarly proportioned cabinet on the other side. The mirrored door at the top opens to reveal shelves, and the flap below drops down to provide a working surface with pigeonholes behind. In the base there are five drawers.

Below: An American oak desk, c. 1900. This large piece was designed by Frank Lloyd Wright for a house in Kankakee, Illinois. Its broad overhanging top is 7ft 8in long, and supported on two pedestals of three drawers each.

ready than their European counterparts to accept plain and simple 'non-style' which owed no debt to history and evoked the rugged life of the early settlers. Stickley's United Craftsmen company prospered and expanded ,but it also attracted competitors and eventually went bankrupt in 1916 having opened large offices and showrooms in New York.

FRANK LLOYD WRIGHT

Frank Lloyd Wright (1867–1959) was arguably the most famous American architect of the twentieth century. Wright's body of work covered many periods, stretching from Victorian styles up to twentieth century postwar designs. He took great care in commissioning furniture to fill the rooms he designed. Wright felt that architecture and furniture were an integral whole, and he occasionally made pieces in the same shape as the buildings they were placed in. He was much influenced by Charles Rennie Mackintosh and was just as innovative. Wright generally made use of massive rectangular forms, carefully balanced one against another, and was influence both in choice of material and simplicity of design by the Arts and Craft Movement.

Wright was equally at home designing for the home as the office. For one house, designed for Francis W. Little at Peoria Illinois, he insisted on designing furniture to complement his architectural style. The whole is neat and sedate to fit with Wright's decorative scheme for the house.

Frank Lloyd Wright's sheet metal desks designed for the Larkin building in Buffalo New York in 1904 were an early intimation of the shape of things to come. Wright's air-conditioned building. with its central open hall lit by skylights was an avant-garde design that was matched by equally innovative office furniture. The metal desks were built with efficiency in mind; there are banks of pigeon-holes for filing along the back, and an integral swivel chair without legs which can be

easily pushed back and forth to make office cleaning easier. The design set a precedent for the use of metal furniture and for the creation of a single system for the entire office, which were to become standard later in the century. These desks, along with the more aesthetically pleasing wood and tubular steel desks deigned for the Johnson Wax office in Wisconsin in the late 1930s, prefigured the postwar designer desk systems.

Below: A painted steel office desk, 1904. Wright designed this desk for the administration building of the Larkin mail order company at Buffalo New York. The metal desks he produced for the company were designed with efficiency in mind: there are banks of pigeonholes for filing and an integral swivel chair without legs.